ROYAL HERI

Kings & Queens at English Heritage Sites

VAL HORSLER

ENGLISH HERITAGE

ROYAL HERITAGE

Kings & Queens at English Heritage Sites

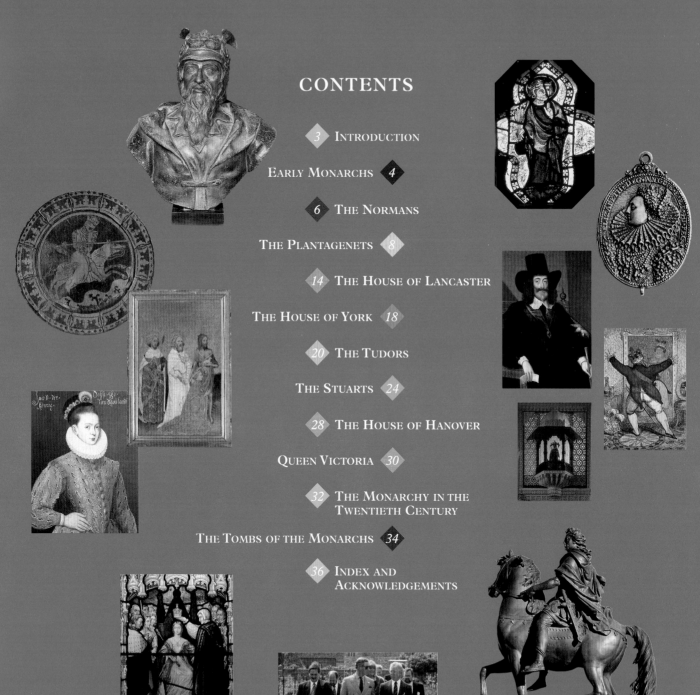

CONTENTS

INTRODUCTION

In 2002 Queen Elizabeth II celebrates her fiftieth year on the throne – her Golden Jubilee. Only four monarchs since the Norman Conquest have reigned as long or longer: Henry III (fifty-six years), Edward III (fifty years), George III (sixty years), and Victoria, the longest at sixty-four years.

English Heritage will celebrate with the Queen, by commemorating her ancestors – the kings and queens of England who built, owned, lived in, visited, were prisoners in, or died at English Heritage properties. Some of these were the places where great events of state took place; others were the stuff of stories and legends; and others were homes or refuges.

Monarchs have always been itinerant. The Queen has four main homes – Buckingham Palace, Windsor Castle, Balmoral and Sandringham – in which she and her family spend parts of each year. In the medieval period, this was even more the case. The demands of war and government required a great deal of travelling, and monarchs regularly journeyed between their various scattered residences with their retinues.

This itinerant royal life is well illustrated at many English Heritage properties. Eltham Palace in south London, before the sixteenth century, was one of only six palaces large enough to accommodate the entire court of some 800 people, and it therefore played home and host to a succession of kings. Edward I often stayed there, as did his son, Edward II. Both Edward III and Henry VIII spent much of their youth there, and Henry IV spent ten of his thirteen Christmases as king at Eltham. But between visits, it would generally have been left unfurnished and unstaffed.

Privacy, for medieval monarchs, was largely out of the question. Courtiers would attend every action, even the most intimate; and servants would sleep outside the bedroom door, or in the room. Osborne House, on the Isle of Wight, presents a different picture. This was the private family home of Queen Victoria, Prince Albert and their children, where they could relax away from the cares and pomp of state. The house is both grand and intimate: the Durbar Room is a monument to Victoria as Empress of India, while the family quarters, including the bedroom in which Victoria died, are much smaller and more homely – though still fit for a queen and her consort.

English Heritage properties feature in the lives of most of the kings and queens since the Norman Conquest. Pevensey on the Sussex coast was the landing place of William I when he invaded England in 1066. Carlisle Castle was a vital stronghold during the wars with Scotland, and Edward I held several Parliaments there. Carisbrooke Castle on the Isle of Wight was Charles I's prison before he was taken to London for his trial and execution. Pendennis Castle saw the flight to France of both Charles I's queen, Henrietta Maria, and her son, later Charles II, during the Civil War. Kenilworth witnessed the forced abdication of Edward II before he was taken to Berkeley Castle to be hideously murdered. Middleham Castle was the boyhood home of Richard III, and Framlingham Castle was where Mary I awaited the outcome of the machinations for the crown after Edward VI died. Many other such connections, both grand and more mundane, can be found in this Jubilee Souvenir.

Left, from top: The coats of arms of Edward I, Edward III, Edward IV and Henry VIII; above: an emblem of Edward IV, all part of the stained-glass windows in the Great Hall at Eltham Palace, south-east London, built by Edward IV Top right: Elizabeth II at her coronation in Westminster Abbey, 2 June 1953

EARLY MONARCHS

It is now generally accepted that King Arthur was a genuine historical figure. However, the medieval romanticisation of his exploits as the leader of Celtic British resistance against the Saxons has made him more legendary than real. Places associated with him in the West Country – Tintagel, where legend has him being born, and Cadbury, the Camelot of legend – were refortified in the fifth and sixth centuries AD, which lends support to tales of a great British campaign, with a major battle victory at Mons Badonicus. But the myths also persist: at Richmond Castle in Yorkshire, local folklore has it that King Arthur and his knights sleep in a crypt below the castle keep. A local potter, Peter Thompson, found his way in and saw Arthur's sword and horn lying on the richly carved tomb. When he lifted the sword, armour clattered on all sides and the tombs began to open. He replaced the blade and all was still. Half-crazed, he fled and stopped up the entrance.

Much of the history of England between the departure of the Romans and the Norman Conquest is bound up with the growth and spread of Christianity. Pope Gregory's emissary, Augustine, landed in Kent in AD 597 with the job of converting the pagan Anglo-Saxons to Christianity, and winning over the adherents of Celtic Christianity to Roman practices. Celtic and Roman traditions varied in many ways, from their differing methods for calculating the date of Easter to their systems of administration. Augustine quickly converted the Kentish king and queen to the Roman way, and his abbey in Canterbury was the burial place for many years of the kings and queens of Kent.

The two rival, and warring, Christian traditions in England were not reconciled until AD 664 when St Hild – a member of the most powerful royal house of the time, that of Northumbria – presided over the Synod of Whitby. Oswy, the Northumbrian king, had been converted to the Celtic form of Christianity by St Aidan, founder of the monastery of Lindisfarne on Holy Island. But his wife, from the Kentish royal family, was an adherent of the Roman church, and their calendars were different: on the day when Oswy celebrated Easter, his wife was a week behind, still only at Palm Sunday. The Synod decided on Roman traditions for the date of Easter and on other matters such as the diocesan structure. Whitby Abbey was therefore the setting for one of the most momentous religious developments of the time, a change which set the Christian church and state on the path they were to follow for centuries.

Several 'Dark Age' kings are linked to English Heritage properties. Oswestry is named after King Oswald of Northumbria, who was defeated

A Victorian painting of Arthur as a baby being handed to Merlin at the postern gate at Tintagel Castle, Cornwall

The beach below Tintagel Castle, Cornwall: legendary birthplace of King Arthur

Right: The crypt of the church at St Augustine's Abbey, Canterbury, Kent

Far right: An initial from a twelfth-century English manuscript showing St Augustine and King Ethelbert of Kent

in battle near the impressive Iron Age Old Oswestry Hillfort, and died nailed to a tree. He was later canonised, as was another king, Edmund, who died fighting the Danes and was buried in Bury St Edmunds Abbey, which became the focus of pilgrimage. St Olave's Priory is named for a Scandinavian king and saint, whose crusading message 'baptism or death' converted many but not all; perhaps unsurprisingly, he himself was murdered in 1030.

It is easy now to forget how inextricably church and state were entangled, and how central the religious proclivities of the rulers were to the government of the kingdom. It is still the case today that Catholics are excluded from succession to the monarchy; as recently as 1978 Prince Michael of Kent had to renounce his place in the order of succession when he married a Catholic. Yet, ironically, British coins still bear the words Fid Def or FD for *Fidei Defensor* – the title conferred in 1521 by Pope Leo X on that (then) staunchly Catholic king, Henry VIII, in gratitude for a pamphlet in his name savagely attacking Martin Luther.

Above: Lydgate presenting his Life of St Edmund *to Henry VI and the monks at Bury St Edmunds*

Right: Twentieth-century sculpture of St Edmund by Elisabeth Frink

Below: Bury St Edmunds Abbey, Suffolk, a place of pilgrimage after the death of King Edmund

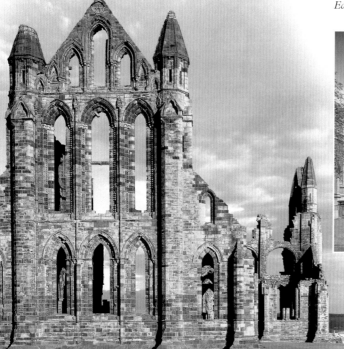

Left: Whitby Abbey, North Yorkshire, the setting for the Synod of Whitby in AD 664

THE NORMANS

Top right: The huge 1820s painting of the Battle of Hastings by Frank Wilkins, commissioned by the then owner of Battle Abbey. It was much damaged by being rolled up and stored for 120 years; it is currently being conserved

Right: The coronation of Harold, as shown on the Bayeux Tapestry

The invasion of 1066 was the last successful hostile invasion of England, and marked the transformation of English society and government as the French conquerors imposed their rule. William, Duke of Normandy, landed at Pevensey, and marched to the place now called Battle where the hard-fought Battle of Hastings took place on 14 October, at the end of which the last Anglo-Saxon king, Harold Godwinson, was killed.

Battle Abbey was founded as an act of penance by the king and to honour the dead of the battle, and the high altar of the church was placed at the spot where Harold had died. It was finally consecrated in 1094 in the presence of William II. It is remarkable that so much of the battle site itself has remained intact over the centuries, so that it is now possible to visit the scene of the ending of one era and the start of another, and to recreate – as re-enactors frequently do – the events of 14 October 1066. As a pleasing coda, Battle Abbey was reoccupied in 1944 by British and Canadian troops preparing for the invasion of Normandy.

Despite the Norman victory and Harold's death, the English did not surrender. It took a march on London and two months of further conflict before William was crowned king on Christmas Day 1066, and three more years before he was secure on the throne. He suppressed the many uprisings against him with great ferocity; and he consolidated his power by a massive programme of castle-building.

Even before his march on London after the Battle of Hastings, William had ordered the Anglo-Saxon defences at Dover to be strengthened by the building of an earthwork castle. Another early royal castle was at York, where the first castle was built in 1068 followed by a second in 1069. These castles were attacked later in 1069 when the local population allied with an invading Danish force to overwhelm the Norman garrisons. William's revenge was the 'Harrying of the North', the laying waste of the entire region, which resulted in a massive death toll from famine and sent out a stern message to other rebels.

William I commissioned a survey of his new kingdom, which went into astonishing detail; the results were entered into the Domesday Book, above

Battle Abbey, East Sussex: the gatehouse and courthouse

Centre: William the Conqueror by an unknown eighteenth-century artist

Above: Battle Abbey and the battlefield from the south-east

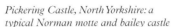

Pickering Castle, North Yorkshire: a typical Norman motte and bailey castle

Some of William's castles were built of stone from the outset, such as the formidable Tower of London, and Scarborough, built on a rocky headland to protect the most important port in the region. But the majority were built quickly using earth and timber. Most of them were 'motte and bailey' in design: an artificial mound of earth, called a motte, supporting a timber tower, with an enclosure – the bailey – below. Pickering Castle was one of these, built by William to control his lines of communication in a wild and unruly region. William's castle-building activities also, where possible, took advantage of existing defences such as Iron Age hillforts. One of those transformed in this way was at Old Sarum where, in 1070, the king finally paid off his troops with Anglo-Saxon treasure – a significant event that symbolised his firm establishment on the throne.

William rewarded his followers with grants of large tracts of land within England, to the extent that, within twenty years of the Conquest, virtually none of the country was in Anglo-Saxon ownership. With the church hierarchy also quickly taken into Norman hands under William's Archbishop of Canterbury, Lanfranc, almost the entire ruling class was French-speaking. Like the king, these new rulers also built castles to protect themselves against the locals. Berkhamsted was a baronial castle, as was Richmond Castle in Yorkshire, which can claim to be the best-preserved castle of its age in the country and boasts more surviving eleventh-century fabric than any other castle.

The early earthwork castles were gradually replaced with more powerful stone edifices, as the Norman nobility strengthened its hold on the countryside and the borders with Wales and Scotland. Rochester Castle was one of the earliest to be rebuilt in stone, probably in response to a failed attempt by the quarrelsome

Odo, Bishop of Bayeux, Earl of Kent and half-brother of William I, to replace William II on the throne with his older brother, Robert. Nothing now remains of the earthwork foundations of Carlisle Castle, built by William II in response to one of many Scottish raids. But thirty years later his brother, Henry I, began to rebuild the castle in stone – a project that was completed, ironically, by King David I of Scotland during the Scottish occupation of the northern counties while Stephen and Matilda were fighting each other for the English throne. David I died at Carlisle in 1153, just before Henry II regained the region for England, of which it has been part ever since.

Henry I, from a fourteenth-century family tree

Left: Richmond Castle, North Yorkshire, built by one of William I's powerful barons to protect his new holdings against the dispossessed English

Below: Old Sarum, Wiltshire: a reconstruction painting of the keep and palace around 1130 by Peter Dunn

THE PLANTAGENETS

After Henry I's heir, William, drowned in the White Ship in 1120, his only surviving legitimate child, Matilda, claimed the throne. Many of the barons, however, preferred Stephen of Blois, a maternal grandson of William I, and the two battled for the throne for nearly twenty years. The conflict was only finally resolved when Stephen accepted Matilda's son, Henry Plantagenet, as his heir.

The dynasty took its name from the sprig of broom – *Planta genista* – which was the emblem used by Geoffrey of Anjou, Matilda's second husband and Henry's father. Even before he was crowned king of England, Henry II held huge territories in France, mainly resulting from his marriage to the wilful Eleanor of Aquitaine, who was eleven years older than him, and had, just before their marriage, been given back her lands in France on the annulment of her marriage to Louis VII.

From the eleventh to the fifteenth centuries, kings of England were in fact French, and, through their baronial holdings in France, owed allegiance to the French monarch. England was only a small part of their power-base. It is significant that William I bequeathed the Dukedom of Normandy to his eldest son, Robert, and England only to his second son, William. Henry II, his wife and three of his sons are buried in France. There is no evidence that any of them could speak English.

Henry II had visited England only twice in his first twenty years, and then spent most of his reign travelling the length and breadth of his holdings in France as well as England. In 1170, he spent only fourteen weeks in England as against thirty-eight in France, and covered over 2000 miles in the course of the year.

Henry I's only surviving son, William, drowned in the White Ship in 1120, when its drunken pilot steered it into a rock

A thirteenth-century manuscript illustration showing three generations of kings: Henry II (top left), his sons Richard I (top right) and John (bottom left), and John's son, Henry III (bottom right)

His first task in England was to subdue the great barons, whose power had grown hugely during the anarchy in Stephen's reign. He built new castles in strategic places, and strengthened many existing fortifications. Orford Castle, on the East Anglian coast, was built to counter the threat posed by Hugh Bigod, one of whose strongholds in the area was Framlingham Castle. Orford Castle is remarkable for its building records which survive in their entirety – the oldest castle of which this is true. They show that between 1165 and 1173, £1413 was spent on it – a huge sum when a watchman received an old penny a day as wages (the equivalent in today's money of £1.52 a year).

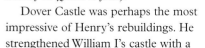

Above: Coins of Matilda and Stephen

Dover Castle was perhaps the most impressive of Henry's rebuildings. He strengthened William I's castle with a new monumental keep, standing at the heart of a powerful ring of defences, ingeniously designed by his master architect, Maurice the Engineer. The richly decorated royal chapel and the stunning royal apartments are still magnificent. Expenditure on Dover Castle between 1179 and 1188 rose to over £6000, creating much of the medieval castle which survives today. Henry strengthened Carlisle too, against the ever-present Scottish threat, as well as Scarborough Castle, his most powerful holding in the north-east.

Desperate to avoid the anarchy which had followed the death of Henry I, Henry II had his oldest son – another Henry, known as the 'Young King' – crowned king twice within his own lifetime. But this did not prevent all his sons conspiring against him, with the connivance of their mother. The older Henry took Kenilworth and Warwick Castles into his own hands as part of his defence against his sons, and never returned Kenilworth to its previous owners. It therefore became a royal castle, and even survived as such after Magna Carta, when it was one of four castles due to be handed over to the barons.

When Henry died in 1189, he was succeeded by Richard, since the 'Young King' had predeceased him. Richard spent less than one year of his ten-year reign in England, preferring to crusade in the Middle East. His wife, Berengaria, never even set foot in the country of which she was queen.

Richard's brother John is best remembered for being forced by the barons in 1215 to accept the Magna Carta, a document which safeguarded the barons' own privileges, but went much further, establishing the principle that England was ruled by law as established by custom and precedent, not just by the royal will – the king himself was not above the law.

John was in many ways a restless and energetic king; he made extensive improvements to Kenilworth Castle, spent large sums on Norham Castle on the Scottish border, and built fine residential accommodation at Scarborough Castle. The residents of Carlisle saw rather too much of him; he visited the city four times and

imposed huge taxes on them. One result was major damage to Carlisle Castle when the citizens made common cause with Scottish invaders in 1216 and besieged the king's garrison there.

John's wars against Philip of France resulted in the loss of half his French territories – the

duchy of Normandy and the county of Maine; and his civil war against his barons, involving his endorsement and later repudiation of the Magna Carta, was to result in important sieges at both Rochester and Dover

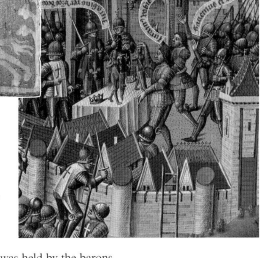

Castles. Rochester Castle was held by the barons against the king for seven weeks in 1215. John personally commanded the onslaught, breaching the south curtain wall and driving the defenders back into the keep. His sappers then undermined the south-east tower with a tunnel

Below left: A decorative tile from Cleeve Abbey, Somerset, depicting Saladin

Below: The capture of Acre in 1191 during the Crusades

Left: An aerial view of Dover Castle, Kent - the 'key to England' - considerably strengthened and rebuilt by Henry II
Below: A Norman knight at Dover - one of the many re-enactments that take place at English Heritage sites

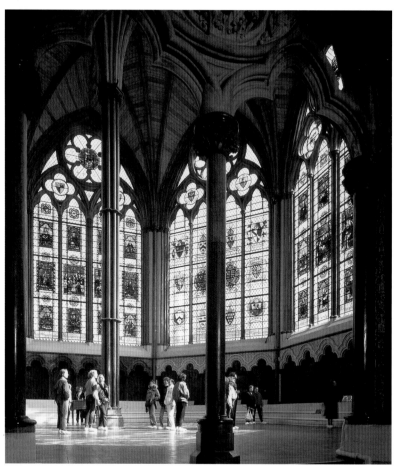

The Chapter House at Westminster Abbey, built by Henry III and meeting place for the first Parliaments; it still retains fine medieval floor tiles, statuary and wall-paintings

Clifford's Tower, York, part of Henry III's major rebuilding of York Castle

held up by wooden props which were then set on fire; their collapse brought down almost a quarter of the keep. After starvation forced the defenders to surrender, John was so incensed at the determination of their resistance that he had to be deterred from having them all hanged.

The siege of Dover Castle was even more dramatic. The rebellious barons had invited Prince Louis of France to assume the English crown, and he landed with an army in Thanet in May 1216. John had barely time to install a garrison and provisions at Dover Castle before retreating to Winchester, and by the autumn of 1216 only Dover and Windsor Castles in the south-east were still in the king's hands. Prince Louis' sappers employed the same tactics as had John's at Rochester, and undermined one of the two towers of the northern gate. Small tunnels which still exist within the castle are probably countermines, dug by the defenders in the hope of intercepting their enemies. This time, however, despite the collapse of the tower, the defenders drove the attackers back through the breach, and Louis called a truce. Dover Castle was badly damaged, but had remained uncaptured.

John's son Henry was only nine when he became king, and his long reign is marked by the beginnings of the parliamentary system, and by the baronial uprisings led by Simon de Montfort. Henry III was a great builder, and was responsible for new work at Westminster Abbey, including the Chapter House which still retains its original floor of glazed tiles and some of the finest medieval wall-paintings and statuary to have survived. During the later part of Henry III's reign, the first 'Parliaments' met in the Chapter House. He also rebuilt the whole of York Castle in stone; work began in 1245 and continued until around 1270, during which time £2450 was spent on the construction of Clifford's Tower and the bailey walls, together with towers, gates, and other buildings. Clifford's Tower, with its four-leaved design, still sits on top of its motte, the most visible surviving remains of the castle.

Kenilworth Castle saw violent action during the reign of Henry III, when Simon de Montfort's supporters in the castle were besieged in 1266 by the king, although De Montfort and his son were already dead, killed at the Battle of Evesham. The castle garrison held out for six months.

Henry's brother, Richard, Earl of Cornwall, was the only Englishman ever to be elected Holy Roman Emperor, though he was never crowned by the Pope. He founded Hailes Abbey in gratitude for surviving a violent storm at sea. Work on the abbey began in 1245, and it was dedicated by Henry III in 1251.

During most of the latter part of his reign, Henry was content to allow his son, the formidable Edward, to rule. Edward left the country for a crusade, and he was still on crusade when his father died. He did not return even for his own coronation until two years later.

Edward I – nicknamed 'Longshanks' because at six feet tall he stood head and shoulders above his fellow men – was a man of achievement. He subdued the Welsh, and built a number of magnificent castles, including Caernarfon and Conwy, to keep them under control. When Edward's son was born at

A statue of Queen Eleanor, wife of Edward I, from one of the Eleanor Crosses built on the king's orders everywhere her body rested on its journey back to London for burial

Caernarfon, he proclaimed him the first Prince of Wales, a title ever since held by the first son of the monarch. He then turned his attention to Scotland, and in 1292 presided over a gathering held at both Berwick and Norham Castles, where he arbitrated between thirteen contenders for the Scottish crown. He eventually favoured John Baliol, on condition that Baliol paid homage to Edward, which he duly did in the church at Norham.

Edward's later defeat of Baliol, and also of William Wallace, earned him the name 'Hammer of the Scots'. It was during his Scottish wars that the Stone of Destiny was moved from Scone to London, where it stayed until it was returned to Scotland in 1996. Yet this fierce campaigner was also a loving husband to his wife, Eleanor of Castile, with whom he had thirteen children. When she died in Nottinghamshire in 1290, Edward was heartbroken, and ordered a cross to be erected at each of the twelve places where the cortège taking her body back to London stopped. Three of those crosses survive, among them Geddington Cross in Northamptonshire, now in the care of English Heritage. The cross at

EARLY PARLIAMENT

This sixteenth-century manuscript illustration shows an early parliamentary session, probably dating from 1278. Edward I presides, with Llewelyn, Prince of Wales, on the right and the Scottish king, Alexander, on the left. The justices and law officers sit on woolsacks, with the lords on the right and the bishops and abbots on the left.

Charing Cross in London – Eleanor's last resting-place before her burial in Westminster Abbey – is a Victorian copy.

Towards the end of his life, Edward again made plans to attack Scotland, and briefly made Carlisle Castle the seat of government in 1306–7 while he was preparing his assault. Parliament was held there, as it had also been in 1298 and

Right: The Holy Blood being carried through London in 1247, accompanied by Henry III; the relic was later housed in Hailes Abbey, Gloucestershire (above)

The Coronation Chair, made in oak for Edward I to house the Stone of Destiny which he had taken from Scotland; every monarch crowned since Edward II has been seated in the chair for the coronation. The stone was returned to Scotland in 1996; the picture above shows it still in situ

An Edward II jug from Brownsholm Hall, Lancashire

Scarborough Castle, North Yorkshire: scene of the arrest of Piers Gaveston in 1312

The Jewel Tower, Westminster, built to house Edward III's personal jewels and treasure

1300 during previous Scottish campaigns. But he was old and ill, and he took himself off, with all his retainers, to Lanercost Priory, perhaps in the hope that the monks could make him well. The priory was almost totally impoverished by this visit. Edward died near Carlisle in 1307.

His son, Edward II, was a weak man, who was heavily under the influence of the insolent Piers Gaveston, whom his father had banished. Edward doggedly protected Gaveston from his enemies, but Gaveston was eventually forced to surrender to the Earl of Pembroke at Scarborough Castle in May 1312, on the promise of a safe conduct. But his implacable enemy, the Earl of Warwick, captured him, took him to Warwick Castle, and had him beheaded. Scarborough Castle is now said to be haunted by Gaveston's malevolent, headless ghost, who seeks to pitch anyone he meets over the curtain wall.

Edward II lost Scotland to Robert the Bruce at the Battle of Bannockburn in 1314, and fled south, stopping at Rievaulx Abbey. The Scots, in hot pursuit, defeated him again at Shaw's Moor between Rievaulx and Byland Abbey, and sacked the abbeys. During his flight, a pendant bearing his coat of arms was dropped from his baggage and was found again many centuries later; it is now on display at Rievaulx.

Edward was eventually deposed through the manoeuvrings of his wife, Isabella, and her lover, Roger Mortimer, whose main residence was at Wigmore Castle on the Welsh border. An illegal 'Parliament' at Kenilworth forced him to abdicate in January 1327, and he was taken

from there to Berkeley Castle where he was hideously killed with a red-hot poker forced into his entrails.

His son, Edward III, was only fourteen when he came to the throne, and it was not until he came of age that he was able to resist the influence of his mother Isabella and her lover, Mortimer. In 1330, he personally took charge of capturing Mortimer and brought him to London where he was ignominiously hanged at Tyburn as a traitor. He imprisoned his mother – known as the 'she-wolf of France' – at Castle Rising Castle.

It was for Edward III that the Jewel Tower was built in London; known as the King's Privy Wardrobe, it was used for some of the king's clothing and his personal jewels and treasure. At this time, Eltham Palace was one of the largest and most frequented royal residences in England; Edward had spent much of his childhood there. Eltham is associated with the Order of the Garter, founded by

Right: Rievaulx Abbey, North Yorkshire, where Edward II fled from the pursuing Scots after losing the Battle of Bannockburn. He dropped a pendant bearing his coat of arms (above right)

Left: Restormel Castle, Cornwall, ducal seat of Edward, the Black Prince, first Duke of Cornwall

The Black Prince died before his father, and it was his son who inherited the throne as Richard II. Richard carried out improvements to many of the royal residences, including Eltham Palace, which he substantially modernised with a bath house, stained-glass windows, a new range of apartments for visiting magnates and new domestic offices. Portchester Castle, near Southampton, had seen extensive refurbishment under Edward III, as part of the coastal defences against the French during the Hundred Years' War and as an ideal mustering point for an army about to sail for France (Edward was there before Crécy). Richard initiated a great building campaign there too, providing a royal palace in miniature within the walls of the castle. This splendid new palace may have been connected with the king's marriage to the seven-year-old Isabella, daughter of the king of France, in 1396, but the abrupt end to Richard's reign three years later resulted in all work being stopped. He was deposed in 1399, just after his return from Ireland where he had gone to quell a rebellion. Legend has it that, before he sailed for Ireland, he hid his treasure at Beeston Castle. He never returned to collect it.

Edward III and his son, the Black Prince, both redoubtable soldiers

Edward III. The king is said to have picked up the Countess of Salisbury's garter, which had fallen off during a dance, and fastened it round his own leg with the words, 'honi soit qui mal y pense' ('shamed be he who evil thinks'). Whether or not it is true that the countess was his mistress, it is intriguing to consider that the origins of the premier English Order of Chivalry may lie in the medieval version of 'no nasty insinuations please'.

Edward III created the first royal dukedoms for his sons. The oldest, Edward, known as the Black Prince, became Duke of Cornwall in 1337 – a title, like Prince of Wales, which has since then always been held by the first son, and heir apparent, of the monarch. His three other sons were created Duke of Clarence, Duke of Lancaster and Duke of York, and it was descent from these younger sons that fuelled the rivalries of the Wars of the Roses.

Edward, the Black Prince, Prince of Wales and Duke of Cornwall, was a valiant soldier who won his spurs on the field at Crécy. He spent most of his active life in France, never set foot in Wales, and rarely visited his ducal castle at Restormel in Cornwall, though he once spent Christmas there. He did, however, carry out extensive repairs to Launceston Castle, and met there with his council in 1353. John of Gaunt, conversely, spent much of his time at Kenilworth, rebuilding the Inner Court in a palatial style, and he also carried out improvements to Dunstanburgh Castle on the Northumberland coast, another of his holdings as Duke of Lancaster.

Richard II, deposed by his cousin, Henry Bolingbroke, in 1399, and – it was rumoured – starved to death

Below: Beeston Castle, Cheshire, where Richard II may have hidden his treasure

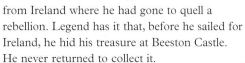

THE HOUSE OF LANCASTER

Pickering Castle, North Yorkshire, part of the estates of the Duke of Lancaster

Richard II (right) yielding the crown to Henry Bolingbroke; from Froissart's Chronicle *(late fifteenth-century)*

Goodrich Castle, Herefordshire

Bolingbroke Castle was the birthplace in 1367 of John of Gaunt's oldest son who was to become Henry IV. He had been banished by his cousin, Richard II, for supporting Richard's enemies, but he took the opportunity of Richard's journey to Ireland in 1399 to land in Yorkshire and reclaim his ducal estates, which included Pickering Castle, before usurping the throne. Henry is said to have first been told of the birth of his son when he was crossing the Wye close to Goodrich Castle, and to have rewarded the boatman who brought him the news with the rights to the ferry. Much of his reign was taken up with wars against the Welsh under Owain Glyndwr, who successfully seized castles and estates on the border. Supported by the powerful Percy clan of Northumberland, Glyndwr proclaimed himself king of Wales and began to make plans for a parliament and a university. Henry eventually defeated the Welsh and the Percies at the Battle of Shrewsbury, at which the Earl of Northumberland's son, Harry Hotspur, was killed.

Henry IV spent ten of his thirteen Christmases as king at Eltham Palace. He built a new set of timber-framed royal apartments there, and survived an assassination attempt there at Christmas 1404.

Left: Reconstruction painting by Philip Corke of the kitchens of Wolvesey Castle, Hampshire (above) during the preparation of a royal feast

Wolvesey Castle in Winchester – the Old Bishop's Palace – was where his sumptuous wedding feast had taken place; and it was also the scene of the meeting between his warlike son, Henry V, and the French ambassadors when – as immortalised by Shakespeare – they tried to buy off his claims to the French throne with a gift of tennis balls. Like his father, Henry V may also have been at Eltham when he learnt of a plot to assassinate him; twenty-eight people were hung, drawn and quartered for the crime. As with Edward III before Crécy, it was from Portchester Castle that Henry set sail for France before his great victory at Agincourt in 1415, and it was to Kenilworth Castle that he retired on his return to England after the battle. He had previously built a new pavilion at the far end of the Great Mere, which he called Le Plesaunz en Marys – the Pleasure House on the Marsh.

Portchester Castle, Hampshire: a major mustering point for armies setting off for France; Edward III was here before Crécy, and Henry V before Agincourt

Left: Henry V, from a fifteenth-century manuscript

Right: The birth of Henry VI

When Henry V died in 1422, struck down at the age of thirty-four by dysentery, his heir, Henry VI, was only an infant. He spent part of his childhood at Eltham Palace, and later made extensive additions to the queen's apartments for the arrival of his bride, Margaret of Anjou. He loved Eltham, and built a study library for his books, with seven great stained-glass windows. This room may have survived a fire started by a lightning bolt in 1450, which destroyed a substantial part of the palace.

Henry VI, enthroned, gives Shrewsbury the sword as Constable of France

Although Henry VI reigned for forty years, off and on, his weak leadership and his frequent bouts of madness led to the increasing chaos and dynastic struggles known as the Wars of the Roses. He was deposed by Edward IV in 1461, briefly restored to the throne in 1470, and murdered in 1471 while at prayer in the Tower of London.

Eltham Palace, south-east London: one of the only medieval palaces large enough to accommodate the entire court, and so much frequented by all the medieval monarchs

THE WARS OF THE ROSES

In the fifteenth century, the laws of succession to the throne were not well defined. The principle of primogeniture – the succession of the elder son and his heirs – operated in principle, but England had no equivalent of the European Salic law, which barred the succession to women. A woman could, therefore, in theory, succeed to the throne or pass on a claim to her descendants. At a time when the great lords were ever richer, more powerful, and often lawless, it was increasingly important that the king should be a strong and effective ruler. Although rank and descent were still paramount, an additional factor came into play: might prevailing over right.

A fifteenth-century illustration of the Duke of Lancaster dining with the King of Portugal

Edward III carried out his dynastic duties by producing a plenitude of surviving sons. But trouble over the succession began when Edward's oldest son and heir, Edward the Black Prince, died before his father, and his son, Richard II, in turn produced no children. The descendants of Edward III's younger sons – Lionel, Duke of Clarence, John of Gaunt, Duke of Lancaster, and Edmund, Duke of York – were therefore well placed to question the succession and to battle for it themselves.

The claims of the Lancastrian kings – Henry IV, Henry V, and Henry VI – came from their descent in the male line from John of Gaunt; but their claim was always shadowed by the fact that Henry IV had usurped Richard II's throne and supplanted the rightful heir, Edmund Mortimer. The Yorkists boasted two lines of descent: in the male line from Edmund, Duke of York, and in the female line from Lionel, Duke of Clarence,

through the marriage of his great-grand-daughter, Anne Mortimer, to Edmund's son, Richard. This marriage produced the powerful Richard Plantagenet, Duke of York, whose son eventually claimed the throne as Edward IV, supplanting Henry VI. The Duke of Warwick engineered Henry's brief restoration to the throne in 1470, but Edward IV fought back and ultimately triumphed.

The Wars of the Roses resulted from the ineffectual reigns of Richard II and Henry VI, combined with the problematic accession of minors – the eight-year-old Edmund Mortimer and the infant Henry VI – and, of course, the ambitions of Edward III's descendants. It saw some of the bloodiest battles ever fought on English soil, and it took a new dynasty – the Tudors – to bring the conflict to an end.

Above: John of Gaunt, Duke of Lancaster

Below: The Battle of Barnet, 1471, where the Duke of Warwick – the Kingmaker – was killed; this was part of Edward IV's campaign to reclaim the throne from Henry VI

THE HOUSE OF YORK

Edward IV with his wife, Elizabeth Wydville, and his son, Edward V

The Great Hall at Eltham Palace, built by Edward IV. The windows are decorated with modern stained glass, including this white rose, the emblem of the House of York

The House of York arguably had a better claim to the throne than the House of Lancaster. Both enjoyed clear lines of descent from Edward III, but the Yorkists' ancestor was Lionel, Edward's second son, while the Lancastrians' was the third son, John of Gaunt. Moreover, Henry VI owed his throne less to the laws of primogeniture than to his grandfather's violent overthrow of Richard II. During Henry's weak and, initially, childless reign, it was the powerful Richard of York who looked most likely to succeed him. The swayings to and fro of the Wars of the Roses, however, left Richard and his second son, Edmund, dead at the Battle of Wakefield in 1460, so it was left to the new Duke of York to claim the throne in January 1461 as Edward IV, and to consolidate his position at the bloody Battle of Towton in March that year.

During this time Middleham Castle in Yorkshire was the favourite residence of the powerful Richard Neville, Earl of Warwick, known as the 'Kingmaker'. Edward IV was the guest of Warwick at Middleham after the Battle of Towton, only to enrage the earl by his secret marriage to Elizabeth Wydville in April 1464, a marriage which confounded Warwick's plans for a French alliance. The king was held prisoner by Warwick at Middleham in 1469 before being forced into brief exile in the Low Countries, during which time Warwick restored Henry VI to the throne. But it was not for long. Edward returned to England in 1471 and began his final campaign against Warwick which culminated at the Battles of Barnet, where Warwick was killed, and Tewkesbury. The Yorkist Edward IV now sat uncompromisingly on the throne.

Eltham Palace was still one of the major royal residences, and Edward IV was responsible between 1475 and 1480 for the construction of the Great Hall with its magnificent hammerbeam roof, which still survives today. He also built a new range of lodgings, and probably also the existing north bridge. At Christmas 1482 one of the most lavish feasts ever held in the palace was given for 2000 people.

When Edward died in 1483, his son, Edward V, was only twelve. The fate of Edward and his brother, Richard, Duke of York – the princes in the Tower – is still hotly debated. But whether or not their uncle, Richard, Duke of Gloucester, was responsible for their deaths,

they undoubtedly disappeared and Richard became king. His short reign, which ended at the Battle of Bosworth in 1485, has left him – together perhaps with John – the most vilified monarch in post-Conquest history.

Richard III, like his brother Edward IV, was much under the influence of the Earl of Warwick, and grew up at Middleham Castle, learning courtly manners and the arts of war. After Warwick's death at the Battle of Barnet in 1471, he was granted Middleham itself by his brother, Edward IV. Through his marriage in 1472 to Ann Neville, Warwick's daughter, he gained the lordships of Barnard, Richmond and Helmsley Castles in the north of England. Farleigh Hungerford Castle, in the south-west, was also one of Richard's possessions from 1462, until he granted it to the Duke of Norfolk on his accession to the throne.

Middleham was, however, his principal and preferred castle in the north, perhaps because of pleasant times spent there as a youth but also as a physical expression of his great Neville

holdings. It was at Middleham that his only son Edward was born, traditionally in the south-west tower now known as Princes Tower; but this tradition may simply spring from the name given to a nearby room on the first floor of the west range, described in a survey of 1538 as the 'Nursee'. Sadly, Edward also died there eight years later after a short illness. His parents were at Nottingham Castle when they heard the news, and a contemporary account describes their reaction as 'almost bordering on madness, by reasons of their sudden grief'.

It is not now clear what alterations Richard made to Middleham, unless he was responsible for the chamber above the Great Hall which was built at this time. But it is certainly the case that Middleham in the late fifteenth century was well endowed with comfortable, indeed luxurious, accommodation, suitable for lords of the highest rank. Richard came less to Middleham when he was king, but his continued popularity in the north – on which most of his influence during his earlier life had been founded – continues to fuel doubt and speculation about his later reputation.

Left: Farleigh Hungerford Castle, Somerset, one of Richard III's possessions

Richard III's coat of arms

Middleham Castle, North Yorkshire, seat of the Earl of Warwick and boyhood home of Richard III

Above: The Victorian painter Millais' famous painting of the princes Edward and Richard in the Tower; their uncle, Richard, Duke of Gloucester, may or may not have had them murdered before claiming the throne as Richard III (left)

THE TUDORS

This portrait, by Holbein, convinced Henry of Anne of Cleves's beauty, but he was disappointed when he met her and referred to her as 'this Flanders mare'

Walmer Castle, Kent: one of Henry VIII's distinctive clover-leaf-shaped castles

Richard III left no son, and so the way was open for Henry Tudor to claim the throne. His claim came via his mother, Lady Margaret Beaufort, who was married to Edmund Tudor and descended from John of Gaunt's third marriage, to his mistress. (All their offspring had later been legitimised by charter in Richard II's reign.) There are few English Heritage properties with connections to Henry VII, though Eltham Palace continued to be a favoured royal residence, and the place where his sons spent much of their boyhood. It was at Eltham that the eight-year-old Prince Henry – later Henry VIII – met the Dutch philosopher Erasmus, whom he challenged to write a poem; within three days Erasmus produced a Latin verse in praise of England, Henry VII and the princes Arthur and Henry. And it was rumoured to have been at Eltham that Anne Boleyn committed incest with her brother, one of the trumped-up charges on which Henry VIII was able to convict and behead his second queen, whose main crime was that she failed to give him a male heir.

Early in Henry VIII's reign, the Scottish king, James IV, was obliged by his treaty with France to march against Henry's forces in northern England while Henry was engaged in an invasion of France. James's forces took the border castles of Norham and Etal, but were defeated at the Battle of Flodden, during which James was killed.

Henry VIII is one of the best-known English kings – familiar for his six wives, his break with

This portrait of Henry VIII by Biagio Rebecca hangs in the Saloon at Audley End House, Essex; below left: Henry VIII's coat of arms, in the stained-glass windows of the Great Hall at Eltham Palace

the Pope and the Dissolution of the Monasteries. He left a legacy in stone as well, notably the chain of coastal defences stretching from Hull to Milford Haven, built in the late 1530s to protect England against the growing threat of a war with Catholic Europe. Notable among these defences are the so-called Henrician castles which used a new design – a rounded, clover-leaf form designed to deflect enemy missiles.

Sandown, Deal and Walmer, the three castles in the Downs, were built at great speed between 1539 and 1540 to protect the stretch of water between the coast and the Goodwin Sands which offered a safe haven to shipping. Sandown Castle has since disappeared into the sea and under concrete, but Deal and Walmer survive in good order, and Walmer is still used as a residence. It was to Deal that Anne of Cleves came in 1539 to become Henry's fourth wife. She was entertained at Deal Castle – still then unfinished – and then at Dover for several days before travelling to London to meet the king. He was impatient to see her, having been beguiled with tales of her beauty and charms, and so intercepted her in disguise at Rochester. He was bitterly disappointed, but it was too late to rescind his offer of marriage to 'this Flanders mare'. The marriage, however, was never consummated and Henry lost no time in divorcing Anne in favour of Catherine Howard.

Other forts built in Henry's reign include those at Camber, Hurst, Portland and Falmouth, where the two castles of Pendennis and St Mawes face each other across the mouth of the Fal estuary. They all bear tribute to the skill of Henry's builders: Portland and Pendennis were

Mount Grace Priory, North Yorkshire: after the Dissolution of the Monasteries a grand manor house was grafted into the ruins

both in military use in the Second World War.

The other great effect of Henry's reign on the buildings of England was one of destruction. His Dissolution of the Monasteries saw the breaking up of many of the great ecclesiastical buildings of the Middle Ages. Rievaulx Abbey which, together with Byland and Fountains, was part of the great Cistercian colonisation of Yorkshire, was left to decline into picturesque ruin. Some church

properties were converted into homes: Battle Abbey, Brinkburn Priory and Mount Grace Priory, among others, all had elegant manor houses grafted into their remains.

Henry's only son, Edward VI, who had been sickly from birth, was only nine when he succeeded his father and only fifteen when he died. The succession was a matter of dispute. Unusually, both claimants were women: Lady Jane Grey, who was the granddaughter of Henry VIII's younger sister Mary and whose claims were forced on the dying king and the Privy Council by the powerful Duke of Northumberland; and Mary, daughter of Catherine of Aragon, who had been declared illegitimate when Henry divorced her mother. For nine days Jane was queen, while Mary waited at Framlingham Castle for the outcome of her counter-claim. Her flag flew over the castle and thousands of her supporters camped nearby. When support fell away from the Duke of Northumberland and his reluctant protégé, Mary processed to London to be crowned. The unfortunate Lady Jane was executed.

Mary was a devout Catholic, and asserted this fact by marrying Philip II of Spain at Winchester on 25 July 1554, with a magnificent marriage feast at Wolvesey Castle. Her reign was marked by the savage reinstatement of the Catholic faith, with hundreds of Protestants burned at the stake – hence her nickname, Bloody Mary.

Henry VIII depicted in an initial letter from the document containing the national valuation of all church property ordered by Cromwell in 1535

Left: The keep of Pendennis Castle, Cornwall, at sunset

Above: Seventeenth-century panel showing Elizabeth I arriving at Tilbury Fort and the defeat of the Spanish Armada

Elizabeth I by Biagio Rebecca: this portrait hangs at Audley End House, Essex

Her husband was frustrated at her inability to bear a child and soon left her to rule alone. She died in 1558 after only five years as queen.

The only possible successor was her half-sister Elizabeth, the daughter of Anne Boleyn, although she, like Mary, had been declared illegitimate. She proved to be a formidable queen.

'I have the body of a weak and feeble woman, but I have the heart and stomach of a king, and a king of England too.' Elizabeth uttered these famous words near Tilbury Fort where she went to rally her troops during the threat from the Spanish Armada. The surviving buildings are later than those Elizabeth would

Tilbury Fort, Essex

Right: Carlisle Castle, Cumbria, where Mary, Queen of Scots, was imprisoned after her abdication from the Scottish throne

have seen, but it was the need to defend the Thames and London from a powerful navy like the Armada which prompted the building of a strong defence at Tilbury.

Elizabeth I reigned for forty-five years, a period of almost unparalleled growth and prosperity in England. A woman of education and erudition, she presided over a time when poets and playwrights flourished, when knowledge grew apace, and when sailors mounted expeditions to the far corners of the world. Moreover, she was the first monarch to – in modern parlance – employ 'spin'. She consciously set out to show herself to her subjects, and she undertook many royal progresses through the country, often to the impoverishment of those whose hospitality she enjoyed. Many are the houses she is reputed to have slept in, and she was not inclined to accept lower standards than were her due. She had no hesitation in roundly berating Sir Nicholas Bacon, the owner of Old Gorhambury House, for the deficiencies she perceived in her reception there.

Many houses were built or refurbished in the hope of welcoming the queen. Kirby Hall was one of them, intended by its owner, Sir Christopher Hatton, as a shrine to his queen; but she never went there. Kenilworth was another; and this time she did grace the home of Robert Dudley, Earl of Leicester – one of her favourites – with her presence, not just once but several times. The most famous occasion was for nineteen days in July 1575, when the festivities included fireworks, bear-baiting, music, hunting, Latin speeches and a play about the massacre of

Kenilworth Castle, Warwickshire (below) was the scene of a magnificent festival for Elizabeth I staged in 1575 by Robert Dudley, Earl of Leicester, and reconstructed (left) by Ivan Lapper

Below centre: Elizabeth I's coat of arms at Eltham Palace

the Danes in 1002. It is said to have cost Dudley £1000 a day, and to have been witnessed by the young William Shakespeare, who used his memories of the festivities in *A Midsummer Night's Dream*.

The repudiation of Elizabeth's 'illegitimacy' had not gone entirely unchallenged in the early part of her reign, and a rival claimant existed dangerously nearby in the figure of Mary, Queen of Scots. Not only could she claim direct descent from Henry VII, in a line untainted by divorce and illegitimacy, but she also had the support both of the French royal house and of Catholics, to whom she was the rightful Queen of England.

She had returned to Scotland after the death of her husband, King Francis II of France, but embarked on a number of foolish escapades which ended when she was deposed in favour of her young son, James, and forced to flee to England. There she lived for nineteen years as the reluctant 'guest' of her cousin Elizabeth. Carlisle Castle was her first refuge in England, but its closeness to Scotland was a worry for her gaolers, and she only stayed two months. While there she enjoyed a certain amount of freedom: she watched her retinue playing football on the green, and promenaded with her women outside the castle walls along what was later called 'The Lady's Walk'; but riding outings were soon stopped because she galloped so fast.

Wingfield Manor was another of her refuges; she stayed there in 1569, 1584 and 1585, and the ruins are said to be haunted by her ghost.

It was not until 1587 that Mary's and her followers' manoeuvrings and plots eventually persuaded a very reluctant Elizabeth that she had to have her executed; Fotheringhay Castle was the scene of this momentous event.

Elizabeth famously never married. And though Henry VIII had been all too aware of his dynastic responsibilities, his six marriages produced only three children, and all of them died childless. It must have seemed a cruel irony that the most logical heir to the throne of England on Elizabeth's death in 1603 was Mary, Queen of Scots' son James, who was the first monarch to unite the Scottish and English crowns. James VI of Scotland became James I of England, and the first of the Stuart monarchs.

Above: Mary, Queen of Scots, who stayed at Wingfield Manor, Derbyshire (left) three times during her nineteen years in England, the last time two years before her execution

THE STUARTS

James departed from Scotland in April 1603, leaving many of his Scottish subjects in tears. He crossed the border at Berwick where the guns of the castle roared out in welcome. He processed slowly south, staying in many great houses on the way, and was eventually crowned king in July.

James was an erudite man – a formidable linguist, an author and a great patron of the arts. It was at his instigation in 1611 that a new translation of the Bible, the magnificent Authorised Version, was published. It was dedicated to the king, its 'Prime Mover', and has maintained its position as one of the seminal works in the English language ever since.

Like his predecessor, James I travelled round his kingdom, honouring great lords with his presence and requiring in return to be lavishly entertained. His queen, Anne of Denmark, visited Kirby Hall for three nights in August 1605, and the king visited four times in 1612, 1616, 1619 and 1624. He and his entourage would have taken over the entire south-west wing of the house, and used it in the way that Sir Christopher Hatton originally intended. But his last visit was marred by sickness. A London letter-writer recorded that he had heard little of the court's tour of Northamptonshire except that 'there be many sick of this spotted ague, which took away the Duke of Lennox in a few days. He died at Kirby…'.

James visited Brougham Castle too, in 1617; the expense of the visit was horrendous. Its owner, Francis Clifford, Earl of Cumberland, laid on exotic dishes of peachicks and quails, and arranged an elaborate masque in which singers, dancers and musicians entertained and praised the king.

James had to deal with continuing religious strife, international unrest, and – ominously – the growing power of Parliament. His ambivalence and ultimate impotence in the face

Bolsover Castle, Derbyshire, where Charles I and his queen, Henrietta Maria, were lavishly entertained in 1634; the banquets included forty-one different types of birds, left

Kirby Hall, Northamptonshire, above, and Brougham Castle, Cumbria, right, both enjoyed royal visits during the reign of James I

James VI of Scotland and I of England, a contemporary portrait by Paul van Somer

of these ranges of threats was recognised both in his own day and later: his contemporary, Henry IV of France, called him 'the wisest fool in Christendom'; and Macaulay, writing over two centuries later, called him 'two men – a witty, well-read scholar who wrote, disputed and harangued, and a nervous drivelling idiot who acted.'

James's son, Charles I, carried on the tradition of accepting lavish hospitality from his subjects. In 1634, he went with his queen, Henrietta Maria, to Bolsover Castle whose owner, William Cavendish, had invited Ben Jonson to compose a masque, *Love's Welcome*, for

the occasion. It was performed in a string of locations around the castle, and was preceded and followed by enormous banquets during which, among other delicacies such as sturgeon, forty-one different types of birds were eaten – thirty each of swans, peacocks and turkeys, ten dozen geese, thirty dozen capons, eight dozen gulls, twenty bitterns…. The tablecloths alone cost £160, and the entire bill came to nearly £15,000 which left Cavendish 'plunged in debt' and gloomy about his prospects.

Charles's twenty-four-year reign saw great fluctuations in the balance of power between king and Parliament, and great devastation in the country as a result of the Civil War. Many castles and strongholds stood out for one side or another. Kenilworth Castle changed hands twice without much fighting; Charles stayed there briefly in 1644. Beeston Castle was besieged for eleven months by the Parliamentarians; the garrison was forced to give up when they were starving, with a surrender which saw the Royalists allowed to march away with drums

The staunchly royalist St Mawes Castle, Cornwall

beating and flags flying. At Helmsley Castle, the eastern half of the east tower still lies in the inner ditch where it fell after being blown up by the Parliamentarians in 1644. Goodrich Castle too was held for the king and besieged. There is a tale of two lovers fleeing the siege who drowned in the River Wye; their plaintive cries for help can sometimes still be heard.

Pendennis and St Mawes Castles in Cornwall were staunchly Royalist. Queen Henrietta Maria, fleeing ahead of the Parliamentary army advancing through Devon and Cornwall,

reached Pendennis in July 1644 and stayed at the castle at least one night before slipping away to safety in France. Two years later, in early 1646, her son, Prince Charles, also arrived at Pendennis before leaving for the Isles of Scilly and then France. Soon afterwards, St Mawes surrendered to Parliament without a shot being fired, since its governor realised that it could not be defended against land attack. Pendennis, however, held out for five months before its garrison, weakened by lack of food, negotiated an honourable surrender and, as at Beeston, were allowed to march out with all flags flying. Both castles were too strategically valuable to be dismantled, so they were garrisoned for Parliament.

When the fortunes of war finally turned against the king, he surrendered himself to Colonel Hammond at Carisbrooke Castle, who was horrified at the responsibility thrust on him. At first the royal prisoner was allowed a great deal of freedom but was later kept in closer confinement in a room on the first floor of the castle; its window can still be seen. Charles tried twice to escape from this room. On the first

Above: Charles I, Queen Henrietta Maria and two of their eldest children; this portrait by a follower of Van Dyck hangs at Chiswick House, London

Above centre: A coin of Charles I or Charles II

Helmsley Castle, North Yorkshire, captured by Parliament in 1644

Right: Carisbrooke Castle, Isle of Wight, where Charles I was held prisoner

Sutton Scarsdale Hall, Derbyshire

Charles II's coat of arms above the gateway at Portland Castle, Devon

occasion he got stuck in the bars of the window, through which he had tried to squeeze in the mistaken belief that where his head could pass his body would follow. On the second occasion, he burnt through the bars with some smuggled nitric acid, but his escape was foiled by Colonel Hammond, who arrived in the room with the words, 'I am come to take leave of your majesty, for I hear you are going away.'

Charles was taken from Carisbrooke on 6 September 1648 for his trial in Westminster Hall. He was also briefly imprisoned at Hurst Castle on his way to London. He was beheaded on a scaffold outside the Banqueting House of Whitehall Palace on 30 January 1649.

The king's execution so appalled the ardent royalist Lord Scarsdale of Sutton Scarsdale Hall that he always afterwards dressed in sackcloth, and after ordering his grave to be dug in the grounds of the Hall, went and lay in it every Friday to reflect on the sorry state of earthly affairs. And as a further poignant aftermath, Carisbrooke saw the death from pneumonia of Charles's daughter Elizabeth, who with her brother Henry had been moved to the castle in 1650; she is buried in Newport parish church. Henry was eventually allowed to join his family in exile in France.

The Civil War did not end with Charles I's death but was continued by his son, the future Charles II, until the decisive Battle of Worcester in 1651 saw the final royalist defeat. After the battle, in his flight from the pursuing Parliamentarians, Charles was sheltered by the family who owned Boscobel House. It was too dangerous to stay in the house itself, so Charles, with another royalist soldier Colonel

Charles I's daughter, Elizabeth, on her deathbed at Carisbrooke Castle, 1650

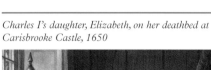

Above: Charles II, a portrait hanging at Boscobel House

Right: Charles II's queen, Catherine of Braganza; this portrait by Huysmans hangs at Rangers House, London

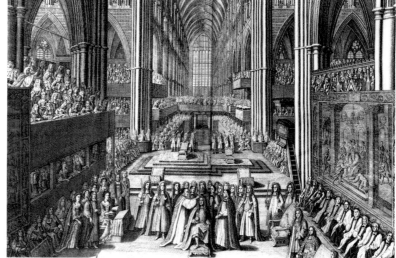

Far left: Boscobel House, Shropshire, where the future Charles II sheltered after his defeat at the Battle of Worcester; after hiding from his pursuers in an oak tree, he escaped in disguise (left)

Careless, climbed into the branches of an oak tree in the forest and stayed there all day while the area was combed by their pursuers. In the evening Charles was able to enjoy a meal of chicken at Boscobel, and was then helped on his way by the loyal Penderel brothers. On his restoration, he granted the Penderels a pension which is still paid to their descendants today, and he dictated the story of his escapade in the oak tree to Samuel Pepys. As a result, the oak tree was commemorated in a number of pubs named 'The Royal Oak' throughout the country, and a descendant of the tree itself can still be seen at Boscobel House. Today's Prince Charles visited it in 2001, after it had been damaged in a storm.

Charles II was very fond of horse-racing, and so he bought Audley End House, originally built for the Earl of Suffolk, to use as a convenient home while he was visiting the races at Newmarket. Thus the house of which his grandfather, James I, had remarked that it was 'too big for a king, but would do well for a Lord Treasurer', became for a while a royal possession.

When the Catholic James II succeeded his brother, there were fears that he would father a Catholic dynasty – fears that looked set to become reality when his second wife, Mary of Modena, had a son. Several leading

The coronation of James II, 1685, by a contemporary engraver

statesmen therefore invited William of Orange, Charles II's nephew and husband of Mary, James's oldest daughter by his first wife, 'to rescue the nation and the religion', and he duly invaded in 1688. James was forced to flee and William was crowned joint monarch with his wife. They were in turn succeeded by Mary's younger sister, Anne, the last Stuart monarch. She had eighteen pregnancies; thirteen of them resulted in still-births, and the five surviving children all died young. Since the Act of Settlement in 1701 had ensured that there could be no Catholic heirs to the monarchy, the succession fell on George, the Elector of Hanover, great-grandson of James I.

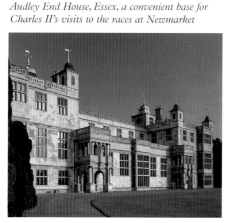

Audley End House, Essex, a convenient base for Charles II's visits to the races at Newmarket

A statue of Queen Anne, in Queen Anne's Gate, London

THE HOUSE OF HANOVER

Prince Charles Edward Stuart - Bonnie Prince Charlie - painted in 1732

Diehard Jacobites still regarded James II's son, also James, as the true king, and there was a rising in his support in 1715. Then later, in 1745 during the reign of George II, James's son Charles Edward Stuart – Bonnie Prince Charlie – mustered his Scottish followers in a doomed attempt to seize the throne. He started successfully, and seized Carlisle Castle in 1745. But his hopes came to an end at the Battle of Culloden on 16 April 1746, after which Carlisle also witnessed the imprisonment and execution of hundreds of his followers. The townspeople are reported to have been sickened by the savagery of the reprisals.

Henrietta Howard, later Countess of Suffolk, was the mistress of George II. While he was still Prince of Wales, he made a considerable financial settlement on her, which allowed her to build Marble Hill House in Twickenham. The house saw a constant flow of society and artistic visitors, including Horace Walpole.

George III's 60-year reign was marred by episodes of 'madness', now believed to have been caused by the hereditary disease, porphyria, of which Queen Anne had died. The Temple of Concord at Audley End was built in 1790 to commemorate his recovery from one of these episodes; and he visited Portland Castle

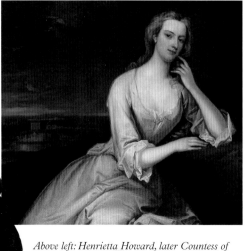

Above left: Henrietta Howard, later Countess of Suffolk, George II's mistress, for whom Marble Hill House (above right) was built

Left: A contemporary portrait of George II

An equestrian sculpture of George III, 1836

Right: The arms of George I above the gateway to Berwick Barracks, Northumberland

Above: The Temple of Concord at Audley End House, Essex, built to commemorate George III's recovery from an episode of 'madness'

Below: A pair of commemorative plates with profile portraits of George IV and Queen Caroline

several times while taking the waters for his health at nearby Weymouth.

His son, later George IV, often acted as Regent when his father was ill. This role gave its name to the elegant Regency style, best embodied in John Nash's splendid terraces round Regent's Park, or in the stuccoed houses of Brighton, the prince's favourite seaside resort. But he is also remembered for his dissolute lifestyle. His long-standing mistress, Mrs Fitzherbert, briefly rented Marble Hill House, paying rates there in 1795, the year of the Prince's marriage. When he became king in 1820, he scandalously excluded his divorced wife, Queen Caroline, from the coronation.

The most celebrated tenant of Witley Court in Worcestershire was Queen Adelaide, the widow of William IV, who lived there from 1843 to 1846. She appears to have been a popular figure locally, and was often seen out driving in her carriage. She had the first village school built in Great Witley.

Below: Witley Court, Worcestershire, home to Queen Adelaide after William IV's death

Right: A bust of Queen Caroline at Rangers House, London

QUEEN VICTORIA

Right: Victoria with three future kings: George V, left; Edward VII, right; and Edward VIII, bottom right

This painting of Prince Albert with Princess Victoria and the dog Eos hangs at Osborne House

Neither George IV nor William IV left an heir, so the throne passed to their niece, Victoria, daughter of the Duke of Kent. Her reign gave its name to a huge surge in empire, invention and creativity.

Queen Victoria visited Walmer Castle on several occasions, the first time in 1835 when she was still Princess Victoria. She returned in 1842, then queen, with Prince Albert and their two eldest children. They were met by the Duke of Wellington, who as Lord Warden of the Cinque Ports lived in Walmer Castle, and they stayed for nearly a month. The royal party were much taken with the 200 ships sheltering from bad weather off the shore near the castle, and took a special stroll along the beach to admire them. Later in the visit the queen and prince, out for another stroll, were caught in a heavy shower and were invited to shelter in a wooden bungalow by the young woman who lived there, who failed to recognise them. They revisited two days later and rewarded the young woman's father, Thomas Erridge, with a small pension.

Osborne House, on the Isle of Wight, was the queen's favourite home, bought by her and her beloved husband, Prince Albert, in 1845. It was a new house, designed in the Italianate style by Thomas Cubitt, with a great deal of input from the prince. This was the home where the royal family could seek refuge from the cares and tumult of government and state, and it was where the queen preferred to live after Albert's tragically early death in 1861. After his death, as the queen retreated into black-garbed widowhood, Albert's belongings were kept as he had left them. They can still be seen today in the

Prince Albert's bathroom at Osborne

Osborne House on the Isle of Wight was a mixture of the grand and the intimate

rooms which served as his and the queen's offices and living quarters. The house is a mixture of the intimate and the grand, with the magnificent Durbar Room – recently extensively restored – a monument to Victoria's fascination with India and her enthronement as Empress of India in 1876.

The Durbar Room at Osborne

Princess Beatrice, the youngest of Victoria's nine children, succeeded her husband, Prince Henry of Battenberg, as Governor of the Isle of Wight in 1896, and often used Carisbrooke Castle as her summer residence. She founded the small Isle of Wight museum in the castle.

Like Edward I, Queen Victoria wanted her love for her spouse to be commemorated in stone, and the result is the magnificent Albert Memorial in London's Hyde Park, recently restored by English Heritage to its original glory. The monument is a fitting memorial to Albert's untiring devotion to culture, scholarship and exploration – a devotion which wore him out and certainly contributed to his early death. His wife was to outlive him by forty years, and it was at Osborne House that she died on 22 January 1901, having reigned for sixty-four years.

Above: The reopening of the restored Albert Memorial in the presence of the Queen, October 1999

Below: A comment on Victoria's withdrawal from public life after Albert's death. The caption reads:

August Personage: What is that large empty building there?
Footman: Please, your Majesty, that's Buckingham Palace

Above: The 1841 census return for Buckingham Palace, listing the Queen, Prince Albert, and the six-month-old Princess Royal

THE MONARCHY IN THE TWENTIETH CENTURY

Launceston Castle, where Prince Charles was invested as Duke of Cornwall

Centre right: The Queen at Kenwood, London

Top right: The coronation of Queen Elizabeth II at Westminster Abbey, 2 June 1953

Below: Portrait of George VI and the Princesses Elizabeth and Margaret with their mother at the Royal Lodge, Windsor, 1940

Royal connections with English Heritage properties in modern times are less to do with affairs of state or royal progresses and more to do with occasional visits. One notable exception was when Prince Charles was invested as Duke of Cornwall at Launceston Castle in 1973.

Edward VII was a regular visitor to Witley Court for shooting parties. Queen Mary, George V's wife, rented Chiswick House for two years, and Queen Elizabeth the Queen Mother regularly visits Walmer Castle each summer, in her capacity as Lord Warden of the Cinque Ports. She also visited Kirkham Priory with her husband, George VI, during the Second World War.

Wellington Arch in the middle of London's Hyde Park Corner is the English Heritage monument that has perhaps the strongest connection with the modern monarchy. It was originally intended as part of a grand entrance to Buckingham Palace, together

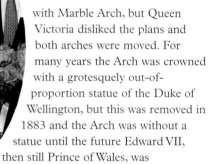

with Marble Arch, but Queen Victoria disliked the plans and both arches were moved. For many years the Arch was crowned with a grotesquely out-of-proportion statue of the Duke of Wellington, but this was removed in 1883 and the Arch was without a statue until the future Edward VII, then still Prince of Wales, was instrumental in commissioning the sculptor Adrian Jones to produce the magnificent *Peace Descending on the Chariot of War*. Edward was said to have taken such a fancy to the young woman who was the model for Peace that he frequently visited the studio to watch the artist at work. His last visit was only a few weeks before his death, when the bronze-casting had just begun. 'I am sorry,' he said, 'for I shall never see it.' King George V and Queen Mary drove to view the sculpture on 2 April 1912, and met the sculptor.

Wellington Arch and Marble Arch for many decades housed the smallest police stations in London. One of the roles of the Wellington Arch officers during Victoria's reign was to sneak the Prince of Wales back into Buckingham Palace after his many escapades on the town. The station always had a resident cat, which during part of George V's reign was a ginger tom called Sandy. Queen Mary's car nearly ran Sandy over when she was returning home one evening, and she was so concerned that she sent one of her detectives over to the Arch to check on his health.

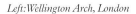

Left: Wellington Arch, London

Prince Charles admires a piece of Indian craftwork, newly displayed in the Durbar Room at Osborne House

Below: Diana, Princess of Wales, and the young Prince William. It is a curious fact that Diana was the first English woman since the unification of the English and Scottish crowns to marry a king of Britain or his heir apparent.

Rather more seriously, Wellington Arch was the scene of one of the few modern attempts to assassinate a monarch. Edward VIII was driving past the Arch when one George McMahon leapt out of the crowd with a gun. McMahon was overpowered and held in the small cell at the Arch before being transferred to more secure accommodation. More recently, and from the dangerous to the merely uncomfortable, Prince Charles took shelter in the Arch, with his detectives, after being caught in heavy rain while walking in Green Park.

For her ninety-fifth birthday, English Heritage built a new garden for Queen Elizabeth the Queen Mother, at Walmer Castle, Kent, her official residence as Lord Warden of the Cinque Ports; she is pictured here in the garden

A recent group portrait of the Queen with the Queen Mother, Prince Philip, Prince Charles and Princes William and Harry

THE TOMBS OF THE MONARCHS

Right: John in Worcester Cathedral

Westminster Abbey is the burial place of most of the English monarchs from Edward the Confessor through to George II, who ordered the sides of his coffin and that of his wife, Caroline, to be removed so that they could lie together as in a double bed. Yet modern kings and queens from George III onward are buried in St George's Chapel, Windsor. Henry VI, Edward IV, Henry VIII and Charles I are there too – Henry VIII with his third wife, Jane Seymour. The exceptions are Victoria, who lies with her beloved Albert in their mausoleum at Frogmore, and Edward VIII who is also buried at Frogmore after dying in Paris.

From the seventh century onwards, Anglo-Saxon kings were buried at Winchester, as were the eleventh-century Danish kings, Cnut and Harthacnut. The bones of all these kings were placed in mortuary chests in the sixteenth century, but four of the chests were destroyed in the Civil War and the bones scattered round the cathedral; they were replaced in new chests after the restoration of the monarchy in 1660. Winchester also saw the hasty burial of William II after his death in a hunting accident – which may have been murder – in the New Forest. His ancient tomb is still to be seen under the tower crossing, in its original position, but his bones were probably removed to one of the mortuary chests. Seven years after his burial, the tower collapsed on top of

Edward III in Westminster Abbey

Henry III in Westminster Abbey

the tomb – the result, many believed, of William's wickedness.

Several of our medieval kings and queens are buried abroad. William I is buried in Caen. His tomb was desecrated first by the Huguenots and later during the French Revolution, and is now marked only by a simple stone slab. Henry II, his queen, and three of his four sons, including Richard I, are buried at Fontevrault in France. John is the exception, with a tomb in Worcester Cathedral. His tomb effigy, made in 1232, was originally the lid of his stone coffin, and is the oldest royal effigy in England. Yet his widow, Isabella of Angoulême, is buried at Fontevrault with the rest of Henry II's family. Eight hundred years after their deaths, Queen Victoria made a formal request for the return of the two kings and two queens of England buried at Fontevrault; but the request was declined.

James II died and was buried in France after being forced into exile. George I is also buried abroad, in Hanover, which he much preferred to his English kingdom and where he spent as much time as he could during his reign.

Edward I wanted his heart to be buried in the Holy Land and his bones to be

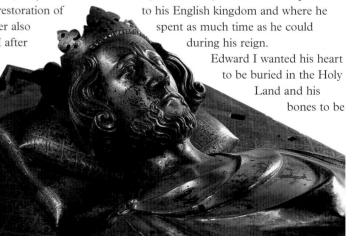

carried on Scottish campaigns; but his wishes were ignored and he was buried in Westminster Abbey in a plain black marble tomb, later embellished with the inscriptions 'Scottorum malleus' (hammer of the Scots) and 'Pactum Serva' (keep troth). In the fourteenth and fifteenth centuries candles were kept continually burning round his tomb.

The funeral cortège of Elizabeth I

and the bones examined by medical experts, who concluded from the dental evidence that these remains could be those of Edward IV's sons. If they are indeed the bones of the two young princes, they suffered a kinder fate than those of their uncle. After his defeat at Bosworth, Richard's body was thrown across a horse and taken to the Franciscan house at Leicester, where it was displayed for two days to prove that he was indeed dead. Richard's conqueror and successor, Henry VII, provided enough funds for a miserly coffin, but this was emptied when the monastery was dissolved in the reign of Henry VIII, the bones thrown into the River Soar, and the coffin turned into a horse trough outside an inn.

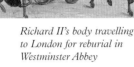

Richard II's body travelling to London for reburial in Westminster Abbey

Effigy of Henry IV on his tomb at Canterbury Cathedral

A few early monarchs were buried outside London: Henry I at Reading, Stephen at Faversham, Edward II at Gloucester, Henry IV at Canterbury. And some were reburied. Richard II's body was moved from King's Langley to Westminster Abbey, an action that failed to quash the persistent rumours that the body was not that of Richard but of a lookalike, and that the real Richard had escaped to Scotland and was still alive. Henry VI, too, was moved from his first grave in Chertsey Abbey to Windsor.

In 1674 the bones of two young people were discovered at the Tower of London and assumed to be those of Edward V and his brother, Richard, Duke of York, possibly murdered by their uncle, Richard III. The bones were placed in a casket in Westminster Abbey, where they still are today. The tomb was opened in 1933

Tomb of Prince Edward of Middleham, son of Richard III, at Sheriff Hutton, Yorkshire

INDEX

Page numbers in italics refer to illustrations

ACKNOWLEDGEMENTS: Sincere thanks are due to many English Heritage colleagues for their help in researching and checking facts, and putting this book together: our Regional Marketing Managers – Louise Dando, Diane Herrod, Nigel Philpott, Estelle Cable, Richard Polley, Nicola Bexon, and Barbara Spearman – for stories and anecdotes; Steven Brindle for reading the texts in draft; Susannah Lawson for her masterful editing and project management; Elizabeth Rowe for scrupulous fact-checking and proofreading; Clifford Manlow for the rich and magnificent design; Elaine Pooke, Richard Jones and Mike Nawrocki for so much help with the production. Huge thanks also to Diana Phillips who came up with most of the wonderful images. Thanks also to Andy Dornan for much trawling through his library, and to David Collyer of the *East Kent Mercury* for the anecdotes about Victoria at Walmer. Much of the content came from the site guidebooks, to which the reader is referred for further information. Norman Davies' recent *The Isles* was a stimulating and fascinating new look, for this reader at least, at the complexities of 'facts' and 'history', and Alison Weir's *The Wars of the Roses* was just one of many books that provided accessible information.

Published by English Heritage, 23 Savile Row, London W1S 2ET
Visit our website at **www.english-heritage.org.uk**
Copyright © English Heritage 2002. First published by English Heritage 2002
Printed by Westerham Press
C100, 3/02, Product code 00019, ISBN 1 85074 818 7

PICTURE CREDITS: All photographs are by English Heritage Photographic Unit, and copyright of English Heritage, unless otherwise stated. Every effort has been made to trace the copyright holders and we apologise in advance for any unintentional omissions, which we would be pleased to correct in any subsequent edition of this book. **Joan Bencowe:** inside back flap *1* **Bridgeman Art Library:** inside front cover, top row *1, 2, 6, 8, 9*; 2 (clockwise from tr) *1, 4, 9, 10*; 8bl, 9tr, 13c, 14b, 16c, 17b, 17tr, 17l, 18t, 19br, 22, 23cr, 24tl, 28l, 29tr, 34t, 35l **British Library:** 5t, 7tr, 8tl, 13tr, 15b, 16tr, 35tr, 35cr **British Museum:** inside front cover, top row 5, 8c, 2 (clockwise from tr) *2, 11* **Bodleian Library:** 4c **Collections:** inside front cover, bottom row *10*, 4br, 11cr, 12tr, 34l, 34b **Corbis:** 3tr **The Master and Fellows of Corpus Christi College, Cambridge:** Cover, MS 20.f.68r 11b **John Critchley:** inside back flap *3* **S. Halliday:** 2 (clockwise from tr) *8* inside back flap *2* **M. Holford:** inside front cover, top row *4*, 6 top inset **Hulton:** 32tr, 33cr **King Arthur's Great Hall, Tintagel:** 4tl **Lambeth Palace Library:** 27 **National Portrait Gallery, London:** 19cb, 19bl, 30t, 33bl **Private collection:** 26bl **Public Record Office:** 6cl, 21br, 31cr **The Royal Collection © 2002 Her Majesty Queen Elizabeth II:** frontispiece, inside front cover, bottom row *2*, 11tr **Skyscan Balloon Photography:** 15tr, 19t **Andrew Tryner:** 11bl, 12b, 21cl, 23b **Victoria & Albert Museum:** inside front cover, bottom row *8*, 20, 11tl **Warwick County Records:** 24tr inset **Nick White:** inside front cover, bottom row *9*